Celebrate Thanksgiving Day

Elaine A. Kule

This is a view of the Macy's Thanksgiving Day Parade
in New York City.

Enslow Publishers, Inc.
40 Industrial Road
Box 398
Berkeley Heights, NJ 07922
USA
http://www.enslow.com

Library of Congress Cataloging-in-Publication Data

Kule, Elaine A.
   Celebrate Thanksgiving Day / Elaine A. Kule.
      p. cm. — (Celebrate holidays)
   Includes bibliographical references and index.
   ISBN-10: 0-7660-2578-0
      1. Thanksgiving Day—Juvenile literature. I. Title. II. Series.
   GT4975.K85 2006
   394.2649—dc22

                                    2005028113
   ISBN-13: 978-0-7660-2578-3

Printed in the United States of America

10 9 8 7 6 5 4 3 2

To Our Readers: We have done our best to make sure all Internet Addresses in this book were active and appropriate when we went to press. However, the author and the publisher have no control over and assume no liability for the material available on those Internet sites or on other Web sites they may link to. Any comments or suggestions can be sent by e-mail to comments@enslow.com or to the address on the back cover.

Illustration Credits: © 1999 Artville, LLC., p. 8; Associated Press, pp. 1, 37, 39, 56, 63, 64, 68, 87, 89, 91, 93, 95, 99; Corel Corporation, pp. 49, 58, 72; © 2006 Jupiterimages, pp. 5, 6, 9, 13, 16, 18, 20, 24, 28, 42, 43, 45, 51, 52, 59, 70, 71, 74, 75, 76, 77, 79, 82, 83; Library of Congress, p. 4; National Archives, p. 38; Courtesy of Gail Propp, p. 80; Shutterstock, p. 54.

Cover Illustration: Associated Press.

CONTENTS

◆ **Chapter 1. Grateful Neighbors** **5**

◆ **Chapter 2. Holiday Beginnings** **9**

◆ **Chapter 3. Cultural Contributions** **43**

◆ **Chapter 4. Thanksgiving Around
          the World** **59**

◆ **Chapter 5. Holiday Symbols** **71**

◆ **Chapter 6. Thanksgiving Today** **83**

Help Out! **99**

Glossary **100**

Chapter Notes **102**

Further Reading and Internet Addresses **110**

Index **111**

Many artists painted their interpretation of the first Thanksgiving.

Grateful Neighbors

In March 1623, Edward Winslow, an Englishman who settled in Plymouth Colony, was traveling to visit Massasoit, a sachem, or leader, of the Wampanoag, an American Indian tribe. Alongside Winslow was Hobbamock, a Wampanoag guide who had helped and lived among the Plymouth colonists, and John Hamden, a visitor from London. They were walking to Sowamet, a Wampanoag village about forty miles away.

Edward Winslow

To Winslow, Massasoit, between twenty-five and thirty-five years old, always looked strong and healthy. Now, however, the colonists learned the chief was dying from an unexplained illness. Following the American Indian custom of visiting the very ill, Governor William Bradford sent

Winslow to represent the settlers. Bradford also wanted to hear about any plans the Wampanoag had in the event of Massasoit's death.

The colonists had reason to be concerned. When Massasoit first met the colonial leaders in March 1621, they established a peace treaty, or agreement. They might have also celebrated the plentiful harvest the settlers had that year, with the Wampanoags' help and guidance. As a result, there had been peace between the two groups. But if someone replaced Massasoit as sachem, their harmony might be broken.[1]

It was evening as Winslow entered the dying Massasoit's home. He cared for the weakened chief throughout the night. The medicine and food revived Massasoit, and four days later, he was well again. Massasoit convinced Winslow to treat the other ailing Indians in the village.[2]

Massasoit was thankful to Winslow for saving his life, just as his people helped the grateful colonists survive their first difficult year in New England.[3] These good feelings inspired the celebration known as Thanksgiving Day.

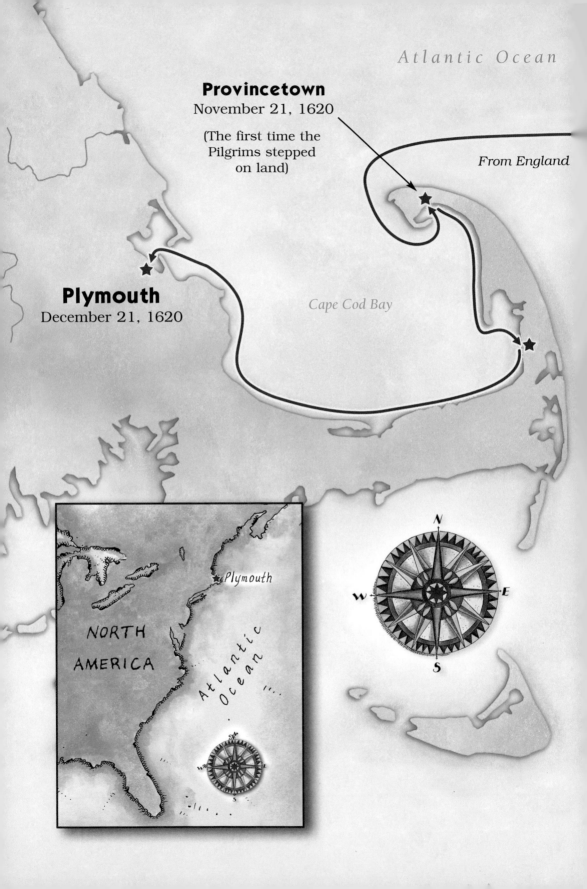

Provincetown
November 21, 1620

(The first time the
Pilgrims stepped
on land)

Atlantic Ocean

From England

Plymouth
December 21, 1620

Cape Cod Bay

NORTH
AMERICA

Plymouth

Atlantic Ocean

N

W   E

S

2

Holiday Beginnings

"Happy Thanksgiving!" is heard throughout the United States on Thanksgiving Day, a holiday celebrated every year on the fourth Thursday of November. At its center are prayers for life's blessings and of thanks for a big meal eaten in the afternoon or early evening. Some people go to a place of worship in the morning to pray. Many Americans say a prayer at the dinner table, before eating. The holiday also honors a tradition that started centuries ago, and the people and events linked with it.

Most of the nation stops work on Thanksgiving Day. Schools, banks, offices, museums, and many stores are closed. Yet it is one of the busiest days of the year, with people cooking, visiting friends and relatives, or traveling to a holiday celebration.

Days of thanksgiving are old traditions celebrated by other nationalities and some religions. Canada has a Thanksgiving Day that falls in October.[1] Many Jewish people celebrate Sukkot (Su-KOTE), to commemorate a time of gratitude for a good harvest.[2] The ancient Greeks honored Demeter, the goddess of grain.[3]

Giving thanks is an old tradition in North America, too. For thousands of years, American Indians have expressed their gratitude for nature's gifts and their families' good fortune.[4] Early explorers and settlers held several thanksgiving ceremonies: in Texas, in 1541; in Maine, in 1607; and in Virginia, in 1610 and 1619.[5]

To trace the beginnings of Thanksgiving Day, let us visit England in the early 1600s, when a group of people were mistreated because of their religious beliefs. Their reaction started a chain of events that helped develop a nation, and a holiday.

England in the 1600s

In the early 1600s, the Church of England, a form of Protestantism, was the official religion of that country. The Church was led by whomever was the ruler at that time. During this time, the ruler was King James I.[6]

Many people called Puritans wanted changes that would purify, or cleanse, Church practices. They felt the Church of England was too similar to the Roman Catholic faith, from which Protestantism had broken away. A high standard of morality was important to the Puritans, who, among other things, shunned sports and games on Sunday. Still, the group believed that changes could be made from within the Church of England.

Some Puritans were still unhappy. They disliked the rituals of the Church, but instead of trying to change it, they chose to separate from it and form their own religion. These people were called Separatists. They were also called Brownists, after Robert Browne, one of their leaders.

Although Robert Browne was not licensed to preach, he spoke to his many followers about their shared beliefs. The Church and the English government thought his speeches were offensive, especially because he was not ordained. They believed his published work was dangerous to the Church and eventually it was banned in England. Two men who distributed Browne's material were burned at the stake.[7]

Since any action against the Church of England was forbidden, Separatist meetings were made unlawful in England, too. As a result, services were often held in people's homes.

William Brewster, a postmaster in Scrooby, England, was a strong follower of the faith and had spoken at or led Separatist meetings. In 1606, pastor Richard Clifton, Clifton's assistant John Robinson, and fellow Separatist William Bradford created a Separatist group in Scrooby. Two years later, to avoid certain arrest, they sailed to Amsterdam, Holland, a country known for its religious tolerance.[8] But the group was caught and sent back to England.

After time in prison, the congregation left England and settled in Leiden, Holland. But the Separatists had trouble there, too. As foreigners, they could not buy land or work in higher paying jobs. King James was pressuring Holland, England's ally, to persecute, or be cruel to, the Separatists. Dutch soldiers destroyed their property, including their printing presses, and threw rocks at some of them.

These people are praying that the passengers have a safe voyage.

The Separatists also worried that their children were losing their English identity. The parents never did grow accustomed to the Dutch language and feared their youngsters were sounding more like Dutch children than English. It was time to find a new home.[9]

America seemed promising to the Separatists. They could have more freedom and perhaps earn more money and a better way of life. John Carver, a deacon, or spiritual leader of the Separatist church, asked members of a business group, Virginia Company of Plymouth, or Plymouth Company, for help in funding the journey.[10]

These wealthy people, who included royalty, wanted to build trading colonies, communities that were still owned by England. The first settlement in colonial America had already been established in southern Virginia in 1607. It was called Jamestown, in honor of the English king. John Smith, an English captain and explorer, led the colony.[11]

The Plymouth Company was interested in building another settlement in what was then called northern Virginia, an area that extended far along America's east coast. In 1614, the men asked Smith, who had returned to England years before, to explore the territory, mostly to find and return furs and other valuables such as gold and copper. Smith later called the region New England, and named the western shore of Cape Cod Bay "Plimoth." He drew a map of the area and spoke well of it.[12]

In 1620, a group of about seventy business leaders, headed by Sir Ferdinando Gorges, renamed Plymouth Company "the Council for New England." Gorges went on a scouting trip to New England and liked what he saw. He and his men agreed to help the Separatists, who promised to repay the loan in seven years.[13]

On the *Mayflower*

Separatists who could afford the voyage prepared to leave Holland for America with money borrowed from the officials. Others had to stay behind and wait until they had enough money for their passage.

William Bradford, one of the Separatist leaders, and his wife were among those moving to America. In July 1620, they boarded a ship the group bought called the *Speedwell.* It sailed from Holland to Southampton, England, where more Separatists came onboard.

Several other passengers, unknown to the group, were craftsmen and soldiers. The business-men hired them to build and protect the new settlement. Captain Miles Standish led the soldiers. These people also hoped to earn money in America by selling crops and trading goods. Bradford called the forty-one Separatist passengers "Saints" and the second group "Strangers."

In September 1620, the *Speedwell* and another ship, the *Mayflower*, set sail. Shortly after-ward, a leak in the *Speedwell* forced the two

The voyagers sailed on the *Mayflower* and arrived in New England more than two months later.

vessels to return to England. Everyone then crowded onto the ninety-foot *Mayflower* and left again from Plymouth, England. Christopher Jones, the *Mayflower*'s captain and part owner, and pilot Robert Coppin, headed the ship's crew of twenty-five men.

The weather was good at first, but then it turned stormy. Waves rocked the *Mayflower* across the Atlantic Ocean, making the sixty-six-day journey very difficult. Many people became seasick from the boat's rolling motion. In addition, with

102 people on board, the overcrowded conditions made the trip very unpleasant.[14]

Many historians believe that navigation errors and strong winds drove the *Mayflower* off-course. Other people think that perhaps some Separatists bribed the captain to sail to New England because the king already claimed the northern Virginia region. They hoped to avoid his control and wanted a place where they could be more independent. They already had a map of the area.

More likely, the travelers were tired and afraid of the bad weather. They were eager to settle at the first place that seemed promising.

When the *Mayflower* reached Cape Cod, Massachusetts, the "Strangers" saw that they were on territory where they did not have permission to settle. Because they were out of the allowed region, they worried that they might have to live by the Separatists' rules. To please the "Strangers," Bradford and the other "Saints" decided an agreement of government should be made for the group.[15]

The voyagers explored the area. For several weeks, groups of them boarded a small boat called a shallop that was on the *Mayflower*. They traveled around the coast of Cape Cod Bay while the other passengers stayed on the ship.

The men took a small boat and traveled along the shore of Cape Cod Bay.

One day, a group led by Miles Standish found small areas encircled by stones. After some digging, they discovered woven bags of corn stored underground.

The corn belonged to people of the Wampanoag tribe. It was their food for the winter and meant to last until the next harvest. The corn was also seed for next spring's planting. The Englishmen took the corn for themselves.[16]

The explorers also found graves decorated with special ornaments and took those items, too. When the Wampanoag discovered these losses, they were furious. Some historians, however, believe that the English later repaid the Wampanoag for the corn.[17]

Noting the region's poor soil and lack of fresh water, the group returned to the *Mayflower* and sailed on. During a snowstorm on December 21,

The Mayflower Compact

On November 21, forty-one male passengers, including four servants, signed a document that was later named the Mayflower Compact. It established a system of self-government that called for an elected leader, or governor. It also included the idea of creating "just and equal laws," for holding yearly elections, and for charging taxes from each settler. It was the first written constitution in North America.

The document was also significant for separating church and state, a key feature of future lawmaking in America. No church leaders would hold political office, and no government leaders would run the church. Efforts at fairness, however, were applied to white adult males only. John Carver was elected the first governor of the second English settlement, or colony, in America.[18]

The travelers decided to stay in this new land.

1620, a group of the travelers took shelter on an island near a place Captain Smith named Plimoth on his map.

The Englishmen saw a stream with clean water, a harbor, some cleared land, and planted corn. The site had been an American Indian village called Patuxet, which means "Place of the Little Falls" in the Algonquin language. Three or four years before, an outbreak of smallpox, carried by European explorers, had killed the otherwise healthy people there.[19]

On the day the travelers visited the land, they did not see anyone else. They thought the vacant area would suit them perfectly. They returned to the shallop and told the others about their new homeland.

On December 26, the *Mayflower* sailed across Cape Cod Bay. According to legend, the travelers landed near a huge rock on the shore of Plymouth, Massachusetts. It was later called Plymouth Rock. It was thought to be where the settlers first stepped onshore, but because no mention of a rock was ever recorded, the event seems fictional. That they were near it is more likely.[20]

The Plymouth Colony

The voyagers were weak from their long, difficult journey. They were also very hungry. Much of the food they brought with them had already been eaten. The seeds for wheat they took from England did not grow in the rocky soil. They also did not know enough about the region to help them get food. Although most of the settlers were not experienced farmers, they knew it was too late in the year for planting.

Women and children slept on the *Mayflower* until homes were built. But when the buildings were set up, they did not keep out the cold. After the first few months of their arrival, people died of pneumonia or starvation. Others developed scurvy, a disease caused by a lack of vitamin C in the body.

The fifty-two people who survived were determined to stay in America. When the *Mayflower* made its return to England in April 1621, no colonists were onboard.[21]

The newcomers soon learned they were not alone in the area. Sometimes they heard loud cries and saw smoke in the distance. Another time Captain Jones and others spotted two American Indians in a canoe. But the pair sailed off quickly.[22]

The people the colonists saw were members of the Wampanoag tribe living in a nearby village called Meeshawm. Their experiences with Europeans had not been good, but this was the first time they saw a group who had women and children with them. The Wampanoag may have thought this was a good sign that these newcomers wanted peace.

It was important for the Wampanoag to find out. Their enemies to the west, a tribe called Narragansett, were outnumbering them and had threatened some of the thirty Wampanoag villages in the area. The Wampanoag heard gunshots now and then and realized that the Europeans owned powerful weapons. They may have thought a friendship with the newcomers would help in case war did break out with the Narragansett.[23]

The settlers wanted to befriend their neighbors, too. They wanted safety for their families and their property. Also, the Separatists hoped to teach the Wampanoag their religion and convert, or change, them to the Separatists' beliefs.

One day in March 1621, a Wampanoag called Samoset walked into their settlement. At first the colonists were frightened, until he said, "Welcome!" Samoset had learned some English from fishermen he met along the New England shore. Samoset told the settlers that it seemed okay to him that they settle in Plymouth, because its earlier residents died years before.

After staying the night, Samoset later brought Tisquantum, a fellow tribesman who spoke English very well. He also knew the area because he lived there years before. He offered to help the grateful settlers, who called him Squanto.

The Wampanoag

The Wampanoag lived in southeastern New England for over ten thousand years. In their Algonquian language, Wampanoag means "People of the First Light." They were expert farmers,

Squanto

Squanto was born in approximately 1585. He was a member of the Patuxet tribe, who lived in what is now Plymouth. Years before, Squanto befriended a British explorer, Captain John Weymouth, and went with him on several trips across the Atlantic Ocean.

Squanto was among twenty American Indians captured by English fishermen, led by Thomas Hunt. He planned to sell them as slaves in Spain. On the way there, Squanto escaped to England by jumping overboard. He lived in that country for years and learned to speak English very well.

Squanto helped the settlers by showing them what foods grew in the region and how to farm them.

After spending time in Newfoundland, Canada, Squanto returned to Cape Cod with explorer Thomas Dermer in 1619. He was shocked to discover that smallpox killed nearly the entire Patuxet community. Those who survived the disease left the village and joined the Wampanoag tribe nearby. Squanto moved there, too.

fishermen, and hunters, and always said prayers of thanks for any living thing they used to survive.

Although it was the Wampanoag practice to help others whenever possible, they grew to distrust the Europeans who came their way. Since the 1500s, Europeans traveling along the shore grabbed many Wampanoag and sold them as slaves. These explorers also carried diseases such as smallpox, which spread among the villagers and killed thousands of them. In 1600, about twelve thousand Wampanoag lived in the New England region. By 1620, less than two thousand remained.

Squanto arranged a meeting between Governor Carver and the leader of his Wampanoag village, Massasoit. Although the two groups did not trust each other completely, Squanto helped organize a peace treaty between them. Massasoit promised that his tribe would not harm the colonists for as long as he lived. Carver said the settlers would protect the Wampanoag and their rights. The two leaders exchanged gifts in honor of their new partnership.[24]

Squanto spent several months as a guest at William Bradford's home while teaching the settlers how to survive. He showed them where to hunt and fish. He demonstrated how burying small dead fish called herring enriches the soil.

Under his guidance, the settlers planted and cared for corn, pumpkins, squash, and beans.

The corn, which the English called Indian corn, or maize, was important to the Wampanoag and the settlers' diet. Its hard kernels of red, black, and yellow were used in cooking porridge, pudding, and other foods. It was not found in Europe, where "corn" meant wheat, rye, and barley.

Squanto also taught the settlers how to tap trees for maple sugar and how to dig and cook clams. He probably showed the children—nine girls and fifteen boys—where to gather berries, and which ones were okay to eat.

The colonists learned how to store food for the winter by packing fish in salt and curing meat over smoky fires. Squanto also taught the English how to build stronger homes using birch bark and trunks from elm trees that would help keep out the cold air.[25]

On a warm April day, Carver fell ill while working in the fields. He died moments later. He was about forty-five years old. The wise and kind leader had done much to help the colonists adjust to their new surroundings, and they felt their great loss. But a new person had to be selected quickly to lead them.

William Bradford was a good choice. Religious and fair-minded, he appealed to the Saints and the Strangers. Bradford was elected the second governor of the colony.[26]

The 1621 Celebration at Plymouth

The harvest was rich that fall. Corn was especially plentiful. The settlers felt they had much to be grateful for, and they wanted to celebrate. Governor Bradford asked four men to hunt for ducks and geese—abundant in the region that time of year—for a feast.

Although historians are unsure about the exact date the festival was held, they know it was not America's "first Thanksgiving," which was what people called the event generations later. Bradford was probably following an English celebration called a harvest home festival that was usually held each year in farming communities. During that time, people relaxed after gathering crops. They enjoyed the results of their hard work with food and entertainment shared among family and friends.

Many historians agree that the 1621 event was not a traditional day of thanksgiving as the Puritans practiced it. In their religion, days of

This is one artist's interpretation of the festival celebrated in 1621 between the colonists and the Wampanoag tribe.

thanksgiving were more about prayer and fasting, or not eating. They were usually held after a drought or a victorious battle.

Two reports written by Bradford and colonist Edward Winslow do not mention any fasting near this time. Winslow wrote a letter to a friend in England in 1621, which was published in the book, *Mourt's Relation* the following year. Centuries afterward, the staff at Plimoth Plantation, a museum dedicated to early colonial history in Plymouth, updated the spelling of certain words and changed some phrases to make the text easier to read. Although there may have been a grateful prayer before eating, the occasion was clearly a harvest celebration among family and friends.

> Our harvest being gotten in, our Governor sent four men hunting wild fowl, so that we might have a special celebration together, after we had brought in our crops. Those four in one day killed as much wild fowl that it and some other food served the community almost a week. At that time, along with other recreations, we practiced shooting our muskets [guns]. Many of the Wampanoag came to the town including their leader, Massasoit, with about ninety men, whom for three days we entertained and feasted. And they went out and killed five deer which they brought to the plantation and presented to Governor Bradford and Captain Standish and others.[27]

Many historians believe that Massasoit and ninety of his men appeared unexpectedly that day in 1621. Far outnumbering the male colonists, they may have heard gunshots and came to the settlement out of concern and curiosity. They also may have been there for a serious discussion about land rights.[28]

The colonists may have been worried in the beginning, but they asked the Wampanoag to stay and enjoy their feast with them. The visitors clearly accepted the invitation. To share in the celebration, Massasoit and his group left the settlement and returned with five deer. Other foods at the table were ducks, geese, corn boiled and dried into a porridge, and a cooked, mashed pumpkin dish called pompion. Carrots, grapes, and nuts may also have been served.[29]

Historians think that, although turkeys were brought to the 1621 event, there is no proof they were eaten. With the exception of deer and wildfowl (geese and ducks), it is uncertain what was enjoyed that day, only that there was enough for the three-day festival.[30]

Food was cooked outdoors over an open fire. Because thirteen women died that winter, it has been said that only four women did most of the cooking. Younger children, servants, and some men almost certainly helped them.[31]

People used knives, spoons, and their fingers to eat. There is no evidence that forks were available in the colony.[32]

The fifty-one settlers at the 1621 harvest celebration were all *Mayflower* passengers. No other colonists arrived from England until after that event.

Other Celebrations

Because there was little rainfall the following year, the Plymouth settlers had a poor crop. Also, thirty-five more colonists had arrived from England, and there was not as much food for everyone.

In 1623, a hot, dry spring and summer ruined the crops. Governor Bradford ordered the settlers to pray and fast. Shortly afterward, rain arrived in time to save the harvest. "To celebrate, it was proclaimed that November 29 of that year was a day of thanksgiving, the first the English ever recorded in America."[33] Still, the colonists did not consider having an annual holiday.

Trouble occurred in the Massachusetts Bay Colony in Boston in 1636. Thousands of new-comers had moved in, upsetting an American Indian tribe there called the Pequot. War broke out. The colonists won, and Governor Winthrop announced a day of thanksgiving to honor the victory.[34]

Over time, there were harvest celebrations, but they were not held yearly. Church services and family dinners marked these special events.

No observances were held in 1675 because of a tragedy called King Philip's War. Aside from costing the settlers and the American Indians huge losses in lives and property, it destroyed their already fragile relationship.

King Philip's War (1675–1676)

Wampanoag chief Massasoit had two sons, Wamsutta and Metacom. Wamsutta took his father's position after he died in 1661. He asked Plymouth officials to give English names to him and his brother. Wamsutta hoped the change would somehow improve their relationship with the colonists. Wamsutta was given the name Alexander. Metacom received the name Philip.

When the colonists learned that Alexander had a meeting with the Narragansett, the colonists thought trouble might be brewing. Josiah Winslow, Edward's grown son, and other men were told to kidnap Alexander and force him to discuss any upcoming plans he may have with the other tribe.

After the kidnapping, Alexander fell ill, and died suddenly and mysteriously. Some people, including Philip, thought the healthy man was poisoned by the English.[35] After Philip took over, the colonists called him King Philip, because they felt he had the same proud manner of a British ruler.[36]

Philip and his tribe were very resentful of the colonists. A growing number of newcomers had arrived in the area and were taking up more land.

On June 20, 1675, in the colonial town of Swansea, John Salisbury killed an American Indian he found stealing his cattle. The next day, Philip and his men killed seven colonists. King Philip's War had begun.[37]

Many American Indians who had been converted to Christianity by religious settlers helped the colonists. They remembered the terrible losses the Pequot tribe suffered from the English in 1636. They hoped that switching sides would save them.[38]

The Wampanoag formed a partnership with their former enemy, the Narragansett. In December 1675, the settlers defeated the Narragansett in a terrible battle called the Great Swamp Fight. It occurred in Rhode Island, where over a hundred tribesmen and between three hundred and one thousand of their women and children were killed.[39]

A Christian Indian named Alderman, who fought alongside Philip at first, killed him in August 1676. Philip's body was chopped and his head was sent to Plymouth. It was kept on display for over twenty years.[40]

The war ended shortly afterward. Although both sides suffered, the American Indians lost far more people and property. Approximately 65 percent of New England's American Indians died.

The American Revolution (1775–1783)

As the colonies grew in number and population, England continued to benefit financially from them. When Parliament, England's lawmaking body, passed several taxation laws, the colonists became upset. Beginning in the mid-1760s, taxes were put on newspapers, tea, and other everyday items, all without a colonial representative in Parliament. The colonists thought that not having a say in such matters was very unfair.

Most settlers hoped to avoid a war. They were proud of their English heritage and enjoyed trading with their mother country. But they also liked their system of self-government that England was taking away from them. Many people felt it was time to declare their independence and start their own nation.

The ruler then, King George III, was angered by the colonists' disobedience. He refused their demands, including that they not be taxed without a representative in Parliament.

In April 1775, British soldiers were sent to New England. A battle broke out between them and the colonists at Lexington, Massachusetts. This started the war known as the American Revolution.[41]

The Second Continental Congress, America's lawmaking group, ordered that a day of thanksgiving and prayer be held on December 18, 1777. Because of the war, food was not very plentiful. Still, people did the best they could after praying for a speedy American victory.

In 1781, two years later, both countries— England and the newly recognized United States of America—signed a peace agreement called the Treaty of Paris.

The Second Continental Congress announced seven more days of thanksgiving, until Congress, the nation's lawmaking body, was established in 1789.[42] That year, George Washington, the country's first president, declared November 26 "a day of public thanksgiving and prayer." It was the first official Thanksgiving holiday in the United States. During his presidency, from 1789–1797, he announced only one other thanksgiving holiday, in 1795.[43]

In the years that followed, no official days of thanksgiving were celebrated as a nation. Connecticut, Massachusetts, Rhode Island, and Vermont set aside one each year. They were held on different days, but each event was spent the same way. It began with hours in church, then home to a big meal with family. Turkey and roast duck were usually served with vegetables, and there were pies for dessert.

Another similarity was celebrating the holiday on Thursdays in the fall. It seemed that Thursdays were the only sensible choice for Puritan New England during the 1700s. Sunday was for attending church services. Monday was the day after, which left little time to prepare a feast. Saturday was spent preparing for Sunday. Friday was a holy day in the Catholic religion, and the Separatists did not want any connection to it.

But Thursday was okay. It was usually when lectures were held in Boston and afternoon sermons were given. The Puritan leaders selected that day as the best choice for thanksgiving observance. Although days of thanksgiving were held on other days over the years, Thursday became the traditional day.[44]

When people began moving west, they continued to have days of thanksgiving. As more

George Washington's Thanksgiving Proclamation, signed and dated October 3, 1789, is in a collection at the Library of Congress.

immigrants entered the United States, they accepted the traditions of their new homeland. By the mid-1800s, all the northern states had a yearly day of thanksgiving.

When the fight over slavery developed into the Civil War (1861–1865), President Abraham Lincoln ordered government offices closed on November 28

The Civil War (1861–1865) was fought between the northern and southern states. This photograph shows the ruins of Charleston, South Carolina, in 1865.

Sarah Josepha Hale

Sarah Josepha Hale was born in 1788 in New Hampshire. She always loved thanksgiving days and thought the United States should have a national holiday.

Years later, when her husband died and left her with five children to feed, she turned to writing to earn money. Her children's poem, "Mary Had a Little Lamb," was published in 1830. Hale also wrote a novel, *Northwood; or Life North and South*, that had a chapter about a day of thanksgiving on a New Hampshire farm.

The novel's success helped Hale find work as editor of a widely read woman's magazine, *Godey's Lady's Book*. She used that job to publicize her interest in making the last Thursday in November a nationwide day of thanksgiving. She thought it would heal the country, where the slavery argument was getting louder.

Sarah Josepha Hale

for a day of thanksgiving. Lincoln eventually followed the suggestion of magazine editor Sarah Hale, who asked him to set a thanksgiving holiday each year for the entire nation to celebrate. She hoped it would unify a very divided country.

Hale started writing letters to government leaders, urging them to declare a national day of thanksgiving in 1846. She also wrote to presidents, including President Lincoln. He agreed to meet her and eventually granted her request. In 1863, Lincoln declared that the last Thursday in November would be Thanksgiving Day in America, calling it a celebration for a "year filled with the blessings of fruitful fields and healthful skies."[45]

Thanksgiving Day was celebrated at that time until 1939. Many shop owners complained that some years have five Thursdays in November, which shortens the gift-shopping season. To help increase store sales during what was then a slow economy, President Franklin D. Roosevelt moved the holiday to November 23.

The decision brought confusion and unhappiness. Some states still celebrated on November's fourth Thursday, and others kept the holiday on the last Thursday. Also, the change did not increase sales at all.

In 1941, Roosevelt suggested that the holiday be celebrated on the fourth Thursday in November. Congress created a bill—a written plan for a new law—to fix the date.

Roosevelt signed the bill. It made the fourth Thursday of each November the national holiday known as Thanksgiving Day. By law, the date could not be changed, and it has not since.[46]

Cultural
Contributions

The 1621 festival played an important role in shaping early American history. It also brought the development of a holiday that all Americans could celebrate together.

Over time, millions of people from all over the world immigrated, or moved, to the United States. They and their descendants helped develop a nation and enriched its proudly diverse culture.

To adapt to their new homeland, many immigrants celebrated Thanksgiving Day with their families. Some of them added elements from their own countries to the holiday. As Americans, they can observe the day as they please

The wide appeal and many participants of Thanksgiving Day have let it contribute much to the nation's culture. Literature, poetry, art, music, cooking, sports, and other kinds of recreation have been affected by this yearly commemoration of a special time long ago.

Literature and Poetry

The writings of William Bradford and Edward Winslow are the only eyewitness records about the earliest years in America's colonial history. Bradford's journal, *Of Plymouth Plantation*, and Winslow's *Mourt's Relation* and *Good Newes from New England* were published in the 1600s. These works educated generations of people about this fascinating time and were the information from which future material was written.

Interestingly, the word "pilgrims," did not refer to the *Mayflower* travelers until the 1800s. It came from a phrase in Bradford's *Of Plymouth Plantation*: "[T]hey knew they were pilgrims." The term came to include all the early Plymouth settlers, whether they were Separatists or not. Before then, a pilgrim meant someone who traveled far from home, for religious or moral reasons.[1]

Many works of fiction, especially for children, were inspired by Thanksgiving Day. One classic is the short story, *An Old-Fashioned Thanksgiving* by Louisa May Alcott (1832–1888).

The story takes place in rural New Hampshire in 1881, on the day before Thanksgiving, parents leave their home to help a sick neighbor. Their two eldest children are in charge of the house. When the parents do not return by the next morning, the youngsters prepare an unknowingly strange holiday dinner.[2]

Art

Celebrating Thanksgiving Day and its history has been the subject of many works of art. Among the earliest was of Edward

Louisa May Alcott

Winslow, a portrait done in oil of the *Mayflower* passenger, who returned to England in 1646. The painting, done in 1651, was by an unknown

English artist. It is the only known picture of a Pilgrim painted from life.[3]

Pilgrims began to appear in American art by the 1800s. They were heroic and courageous subjects for artists wanting to convey images of a young nation's history.

In 1836, the U.S. government asked Robert W. Weir to paint *The Picture of the Embarkation of the Pilgrims from Delfthaven in Holland.* Officials wanted the art to fill panels in the rotunda of the Capitol in Washington, D.C.

The 12 foot by 18 foot painting took seven years to complete. It shows the Pilgrims gathered around their pastor, John Robinson, for a last service on the deck of the *Speedwell* before it left Holland. The painting is also printed on the back of the American $10,000 bill.[4]

Anna Mary Robertson (1860–1961) was a self-taught artist mostly known as Grandma Moses. She spent years embroidering pictures on canvas until the muscles in her hands could no longer hold the special needles. Moses switched to painting when she was seventy-five years old.

One day, an art collector named Louis Caldor saw her work displayed in a local drugstore window. He bought the pieces and exhibited her pictures at the Museum of Modern Art in New York City. Moses became famous shortly afterward.

Moses drew country scenes based on memories of her early life. Among her popular works was *The Thanksgiving Turkey*. It was first displayed at New York City's Metropolitan Museum of Art in 1943.[5]

In 1943, American illustrator Norman Rockwell (1894–1978) painted *Freedom from Want*. Set during World War II, it shows a woman placing a large, cooked turkey on a Thanksgiving dinner table while her eager family looks on. This and many other works were done for the covers of *The Saturday Evening Post*, a general-interest magazine that was popular at the time. Rockwell painted their cover art for forty-seven years.

Another holiday cover for the magazine was Rockwell's *Thanksgiving: Mother and Son Peeling Potatoes*, done in 1945. The painting shows a man in an Air Force uniform who has recently returned home. He and his mother seem quietly grateful to share the everyday act of peeling potatoes for a holiday they will spend together.[6]

In 1969, Rockwell established the Norman Rockwell Museum in Stockbridge, Massachusetts, where his art is displayed. Because his work became such an important part of American culture, he received the Presidential Medal of Freedom in 1977. The award is America's highest honor for someone who is not a soldier.[7]

Music

"We Gather Together" is one well-known song connected with Thanksgiving Day. It was based on a Dutch prayer that colonists added music to, and eventually it became a holiday favorite in homes, schools, and houses of worship.

> We gather together to ask the Lord's blessing;
> He chastens and hastens his will to make known;
> The wicked oppressing now cease from distressing,
> Sing praises to his name: He forgets not his own.[8]

Another holiday tune, "The New England Boy's Song about Thanksgiving Day," or "Thanksgiving Day," was written in the 1800s by novelist and editor Lydia Maria Child of Massachusetts. It has since become known by its first line—"Over the River and Through the Wood"—and remains a holiday classic, especially among children.

> Over the river and through the wood,
> To grandmother's house we go;

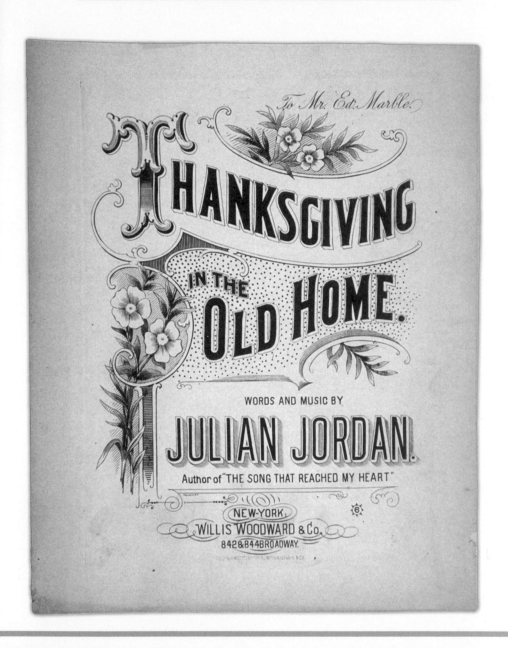

"Thanksgiving in the Old Home" was a song written in 1888.

The horse knows the way,

To carry the sleigh

Through the white and drifted snow.[9]

Food and Cooking

Many foods traditionally connected with Thanksgiving Day were not served at the 1621 celebration in Plymouth. Sugar, for example, was not available then. Items that became part of the traditional menu over time are turkey, cranberry sauce, squash, corn, pumpkin, custard, and chicken pie. Dozens of recipes have been developed for Thanksgiving dishes over the years and traded among families and friends.

Almost all of these foods are a legacy from Squanto, the Plymouth colonists' good friend and neighbor, who taught them to hunt, fish, and plant—and survive. If the weather was good, corn was plentiful and could be made into different kinds of food. Corn chowder, cornbread, and corn-on-the-cob are items still eaten today.[10]

People harvest cranberries in September and October. American Indians taught the colonists how to dry cranberries so they could be eaten during the winter. Cranberry sauce was made by chopping and stewing the fruit in boiling water.[11]

Some English dishes, such as mince pie and plum pudding, were linked to Christmas. But the Puritans did not celebrate that holiday because of its connection to Catholicism. They enjoyed the pie, however, and included it in their thanksgiving menu. Mince pie contained chopped apples, raisins, and sometimes a spicy chopped meat called mincemeat.[12]

Cranberries can be made into juice, sauce, and can also be used in cakes.

Pumpkins symbolize fall harvests and are traditionally linked with Thanksgiving Day.

Plum pudding has no plums. It is a steamed mixture of flour, sugar, spices, raisins, and currants, which were called plums centuries ago.

Other foods came from New England farms that used the preserving methods taught to the early colonists: apple butter, apple cider, pickled pears and peaches, currant jelly, and gooseberry jam. Stewed pumpkin, called pompion in the 1600s by the English settlers, was eaten every day and sometimes at every meal.[13]

Vegetarians—people who do not eat meat, poultry, or fish—prepare holiday dishes in keeping with their beliefs. Tofu—a soft, cheeselike food made from mixing a soybean plant with water—can be formed into a turkey shape. Such practices came into use mostly after 1980 and have gained many followers since then.[14]

Sports

Thousands of years ago, English farmers began a custom of playing games, including jumping and archery contests, at harvest celebrations.[15] It was probably this tradition that inspired the settlers and the Wampanoag to have sporting events at the 1621 celebration in Plymouth. In time, watching or playing sports became part of the Thanksgiving holiday in many homes.

If the weather was cold enough in New England, people went ice-skating, sledding, or sleigh riding. In 1876, college football teams held a championship game on Thanksgiving Day. By the end of the century, watching or playing football on the holiday became customary.[16]

Kids of all ages play football on Thanksgiving.

In Massachusetts, two public high schools—Boston Latin and Boston English—have played football on Thanksgiving every year since 1887.

The National Football League (NFL), an organization of professional football teams, held its first Thanksgiving Day game in 1934. Thousands of fans saw the Detroit Lions play the Chicago Bears at the University of Detroit stadium. People all over the country listened to the game on the radio.[17]

When television became available in the 1950s, watching professional football on Thanksgiving Day became a yearly tradition. Celebrities sing "The Star Spangled Banner" at the start of each game. Other entertainers perform during the halftime show.

The Macy's Thanksgiving Day Parade

The Macy's Thanksgiving Day Parade, held every year in New York City, is one of the biggest festivities of the holiday. It was inspired by the first Thanksgiving Day parade held by Gimbel's department store in Philadelphia in 1921. Three years later, Macy's employees, many of whom were immigrants, urged their bosses to do the same thing in New York City.

The first parade began at 9:00 A.M. on November 27, 1924. It was called Macy's Christmas Parade, even though it took place on Thanksgiving Day. Marchers included nearly one thousand Macy's employees. About 250,000 people watched along the six-mile route. There were clowns, zoo animals, and marching bands. Floats, some featuring Mother Goose characters, were pulled

Even today, Santa Claus is the last float in the Macy's Thanksgiving Day Parade.

by horses. The last float carried Santa Claus, and helped launch the beginning of the gift-buying season.[18]

In 1927, balloons filled with a gas called helium were used in the parade for the first time. The balloons were shaped into popular cartoon figures of the time, such as Felix the Cat.[19]

The parade has been held every year, except during World War II in 1942, 1943, and 1944. The parade was canceled during that time because trucks that were carrying the floats needed precious gasoline. Also, the balloons used rubber, another important material in the war effort.[20]

Thanksgiving Day has made lasting changes to American culture. It has also united the country and its new citizens. They took a chance and made America their home, just as the early settlers did.

For many of these people, harvest festivals or thanksgiving celebrations were not new to them. The countries where they immigrated from have similar holidays, although they may be held at different times, in different places, and in different ways.

4

Thanksgiving Around the World

Even if Americans are traveling or living outside the country, it is likely they will celebrate Thanksgiving Day somehow—perhaps by eating turkey, visiting family, or just relaxing and having fun. They may also stop a moment to think about why they are grateful and say a prayer of thanks.

Other nationalities and religions have days of thanksgiving or harvest festivals. According to

Peggy Baker, director and curator of the Pilgrim Hall Museum in Plymouth, Massachusetts, these two terms have come to mean nearly the same thing, although that was not always so. In the 1600s, days of thanksgiving meant praying all day in church. People fasted if they needed rainfall to break a dry spell or hope a battle would end victoriously. Sometimes a day of thanksgiving came after a good event happened, as a way to express gratitude. By the middle 1600s, community dinners were held at some congregations at the end of a day of thanksgiving.[1]

Harvest festivals often followed a successful planting season and were held after a gathering of crops. They were happy events, filled with food, music, and dancing.

Many harvest festivals had their beginnings in ancient times. In the United States, the Wampanoag have celebrated Cranberry Day for centuries. It falls on the second Tuesday in October and is their most important tribal holiday.

Children stay home from school on that day to help gather the fruit. At lunch, they listen to older relatives tell stories about Cranberry Days of long ago.

That night, the community contributes to a big dinner that they share and enjoy together. Prayers of gratitude are said for a successful harvest. After the meal, people celebrate by singing and dancing.[2]

Many other people have harvest festivals or days of thanksgiving. Some are listed below. Their country of origin is in parentheses, although these holidays may be celebrated elsewhere in the world, too.

Thanksgiving Day (Canada)

Canada celebrates its Thanksgiving Day on the second Monday in October. Its holiday's beginnings started long ago, and like the American Thanksgiving, it developed slowly.

In 1578, Martin Frobisher, an English explorer, survived the long voyage across the Atlantic Ocean to a large island now known as Newfoundland. Grateful, he held a thanksgiving ceremony, and settlers who later followed him kept the tradition.

An official day of thanksgiving in Canada was held in April 1872 to celebrate the recovery of the Prince of Wales from a serious illness. There were no other days of thanksgiving until 1879, when it was observed on a Thursday in November. From then on, the holiday was celebrated each year, but without a set date.

In 1957, the second Monday in October was chosen as Thanksgiving Day. Parliament,

Canada's lawmaking body, stated the nation was grateful "for the bountiful harvest with which Canada has been blessed."

Thanksgiving Day in Canada is celebrated with parades and a big meal. Lamb or ham are usually served.[3]

Autumn Moon Festival (China)

The Autumn Moon Festival is a time to celebrate the bountiful rice and wheat harvest in China. The festival is also a tribute to the "shining harvest moon," when it appears brighter and larger than at any time of year. To the Chinese people, the shapes of moon symbolize family unity and happiness.

The celebration falls on the fifteenth day of the eighth month of the Chinese calendar, or mid-September. It is one of the most celebrated Chinese holidays.

Chinese families commemorate the day with a big meal. Mooncakes are served, which are traditionally small, round pastries meant to symbolize the moon. It is customary for people to give mooncakes as holiday gifts.

Many people buy mooncakes in bakeries or markets because they do not have time to prepare them. These store-bought pastries come in a tin box of four. The boxes are usually decorated with

These women are selling traditional Chinese lanterns in China during an autumn festival.

Chinese designs, and the cakes are signed by the baker. Some bakers are well known and charge extra for their pastries.[4]

Sukkot (Israel)

Sukkot (pronounced Soo-KOTE) is the Jewish harvest festival. It begins on the fifteenth day of the

Hebrew month of Tishri, and is usually held in September or October. The holiday, also called the Feast of Tabernacles, lasts for seven days.

The festival dates back to biblical times, when the Hebrews wandered in the wilderness on the way to Canaan (now called Israel). During this time, the group lived in open huts called sukkot and prayed in movable tents called tabernacles.

Jews in Jerusalem, Israel, participate in a blessing during Sukkot. They each hold four holiday symbols—a fruit called citron, a willow branch, a plant called myrtle, and a date palm.

In later years, farmers lived in sukkot during harvest time and said prayers of thanks for their successful harvest. The tradition has continued among Jewish people all over the world. They build sukkot outdoors—in open fields, backyards, or building rooftops.

The roof of the sukkah (the singular word for sukkot) is made of loosely woven tree branches that are decorated with fruits and flowers. According to Jewish law, people must be able to look up and see the sky and the stars to feel a more spiritual connection to God. People eat meals inside the huts, where they also sing and pray in the Hebrew language.[5]

Niiname-sai (Japan)

While many of today's harvest or thanksgiving traditions began centuries ago, the holiday known as Niiname-sai is rather new. In 1948, the Japanese government declared a national day of thanksgiving or a celebration for a bountiful harvest. November 23 was chosen as the date. It was also decided to honor working people, at this time, too.

Niiname-sai is considered an important holiday in Japan. A big public celebration is held.

For the occasion, the Japanese emperor dedicates that year's rice harvest to the gods and "tastes it for the first time at the Imperial Household."[6]

Yam Festival (Africa)

Yams are a large root vegetable that are the most widely grown food in most African nations. The Yam Festival, celebrated in Ghana and Nigeria, is a three-day event held at the end of the harvesting season.

The holiday begins with a cleansing ceremony to honor relatives who have died. Farmers also give thanks to the gods, hoping for a good harvest in the future. The festival ends with a big meal. Mashed yams with hard-boiled eggs are an important part of the dinner.

Yams are sometimes confused with sweet potatoes, which are grown in Asia. Both vegetables may be seen on the typical Thanksgiving Day menu in the United States.[7]

Pongal (India)

Pongal is a harvest festival celebrated in India. It begins every year on January fourteenth. The celebration's name comes from the word "pongu," which means the "boiling over" of milk and rice in the Hindu language. Hindu is one of the main languages spoken in India.

During the holiday, people gather with their family and rejoice and share their joy and their harvest with others. They wear new clothes and exchange gifts. They also share the custom of cooking rice, dry fruits—such as figs and raisins—sugar, and milk in a clay pot. The mixture is allowed to boil over, which symbolizes prosperity for the coming year. The dish is then offered to the Sun God as a gesture of thanks for a good harvest.[8]

Chusok (Korea)

Chusok is a harvest celebration that joins families together throughout Korea. It occurs at harvest time on August 15, when Koreans thank their ancestors for giving them rice and fruit.

The festival begins on the eve of Chusok and ends the day after. Women cook for Chusok many days in advance. The celebration starts with a family gathering where rice cakes are served. They are made with rice, beans, sesame seeds, and chestnuts. Afterward, the family honors their ancestors by visiting their graves. Rice and fruit are left there as offerings. At night, children wear traditional Korean clothes and dance outdoors in a large circle.[9]

Chusok is a busy travel day in Korea, just as Thanksgiving Day is for many Americans.

English Harvest Festival (Great Britain)

England's harvest festival is called Harvest Home. It usually occurs at the end of September, after all the crops have been gathered. Many farmers use their best crops and flowers to decorate local churches. They also leave offerings of fruit and vegetables on alters as part of a thanksgiving service. They are grateful for the harvest and hope for a good one next year as well.

During the service, farmers sing and say prayers of thanks. After the service, the offerings are given to people in need.

At home, people invite friends and neighbors to enjoy a large meal. Later, they play games and dance to music.

Unlike the United States and Canada, Great Britain does not have a set date for a national harvest festival, but their celebration is always on a Sunday. There is also a parade in the capital city of London, where many people wear traditional costumes.[10]

❖ ❖ ❖ ❖

These holidays share similarities with Thanksgiving Day: a gathering of family and friends, grateful prayers, and a festive meal commemorating a plentiful harvest. But certain symbols are uniquely connected to the American celebration.

5

Holiday Symbols

Pictures of turkeys, cornucopia, and Pilgrim hats have become Thanksgiving Day symbols over the years. Displayed in American shops, homes, and advertisements in the beginning of November, they signal the arrival of an important festivity—Thanksgiving Day.

Turkeys

Turkeys, native to North America, were plentiful in New England and were significant in the settlers'

Turkey has become the big attraction of the Thanksgiving feast.

diet. They were always considered a welcome addition to a holiday table.

But after World War II, the large birds began to symbolize Thanksgiving in a big way. The poultry industry worked successfully to promote the turkey as the holiday's main event. More than 45 million turkeys are eaten in the United States at this time.

The practice of breaking the bird's wishbone, with wishes granted to whoever gets the larger piece, is considered an ancient Roman custom. Europeans who practiced the custom brought it to America.[1]

For over fifty years, the National Turkey Federation has given a turkey to a U.S. president each November. Although live turkeys have been given to presidents since Lincoln's era, the official tradition began in 1947, with President Harry S. Truman.

President George H. W. Bush began the practice of "pardoning" the bird in 1989 so that it would not be killed.[2] An alternate turkey also gets chosen in case something happens to the first bird.

Ceremonies are held the day before each Thanksgiving in the White House Rose Garden. For many years, the turkeys were sent to Frying Pan Park in Virginia. In 2005, the national turkey and its alternate were given a home at Disneyland Resort in Anaheim, California.[3]

Cornucopia

The horn-shaped cornucopia, a symbol of a good harvest, came from Greek and Roman mythology. In the Greek culture, the cornucopia was a horn belonging to a goat who nursed the god Zeus when he was a baby. The horn produced a food and drink called ambrosia and nectar.

In Roman mythology, the cornucopia was the horn of a river god. The hero Hercules broke off the horn during combat. Water fairies filled the horn with flowers and fruit and offered it to Copia, the goddess of plenty.

When European farmers were grateful for a good crop, they filled a curved goat's horn with fruit and grain. The symbol was called a cornucopia, or horn of plenty.

After moving to colonial America, farmers continued the custom. In later years, it became a Thanksgiving Day symbol. According to Kathleen Curtin, food historian at Plimoth Plantation (Plimoth is spelled as it was in colonial times), cornucopias became a Thanksgiving holiday symbol in the nineteenth century.[4]

Indian Corn

The harvest of a multicolored corn called maize prompted the 1621 festival. The settlers had never seen such a vegetable, with its hard, round kernels

Holiday cornucopias can be filled with foods of the harvest season, such as apples.

The American Indians' main crop was corn. Sometimes they dried it and ground it into a powder called corn meal. They would then use the corn meal to make bread.

and smooth coat. Indian corn had been a major part of the Wampanoag diet for centuries and became important to the colonists as well.

Indian corn grows well in cool climates. In the fall, many people decorate their homes and front doors with ears of flint corn. It has been widely recognized as a Thanksgiving Day symbol.[5]

Gourds, Pumpkins, and Squash

Gourd is the name of trailing or climbing plants. Pumpkins and squash are part of the gourd family. Their leaves are large and their flowers are yellow.

American Indians introduced gourds, pumpkins, and other squash to the early colonists. These fruits, which ripen in late summer, became associated with the beginning of autumn. In time, they were symbolic of the harvest festival that became Thanksgiving Day.[6]

There are many different types of squash.

Plymouth Rock

Plymouth Rock is made of granite, a hard, rough substance found on every continent. It broke off from a glacier—a mountain of ice—thousands of years ago. The numbers 1620 were carved into it to commemorate the year the English settlers arrived in Plymouth. But the story of the Pilgrims actually landing on that spot is legendary.

Two books written by passengers describe the *Mayflower* journey. One is Edward Winslow's *Mourt's Relation.* The other is William Bradford's *Of Plymouth Plantation.* Neither text mentions a rock

The story about Plymouth Rock may be legendary, but the rock is a Thanksgiving Day symbol.

in describing their Plymouth arrival. Still, some historians think that the rock may have supported a plank the travelers could have walked upon to get onshore as they left the *Mayflower*.

The rock split during the American Revolution, when it was removed for use as a pedestal. The two halves were pieced together and returned to the bottom of Coles Hill, near the water's edge at Plymouth Harbor. Tourists looking for souvenirs have also chipped the rock.

Experts think the legend of Plymouth Rock may have started in 1741, when a man living in Plymouth, Elder William Faunce, claimed his father told him the rock was where the colonists landed. The story spread and grew more important after the American Revolution, when symbols of liberty became powerful and necessary to a young nation that had fought so hard for it.

The gray rock, about four by five and one-half feet, is protected by a granite canopy, or covering, at the shore of Plymouth Harbor. In 1920, an iron grate was built on the side facing the water, near the canopy.[7]

Statue of Massasoit

A bronze statue of Massasoit, the respected Wampanoag chief who tried to live peacefully among the English settlers, overlooks Plymouth Harbor. The idea of honoring the sachem came from a social organization called the Improved Order of Red Men in 1911. The outbreak of World War I in 1914 stopped additional fund-raising for the project. The work was completed in 1921 by Cyrus Dallin, a sculptor who specialized in portraying American Indians.[8]

Early American Clothing

Children performing in school plays about Thanksgiving Day wear clothing resembling those worn by early Americans. Many adults dress in this fashion as well, hoping to connect more fully with the spirit of the day.

In one large American city, Gail Propp and her family dress in clothing similar to those worn by the Pilgrims and the Wampanoag. The garments were researched carefully for accuracy with the help of an historian from a university.

Propp explains why she and her family wear these outfits each year:

This is a statue of the Wampanoag chief, Massasoit.

The Propp family dresses up for Thanksgiving as a way to make the holiday more meaningful to them.

At first, I just wanted to make Thanksgiving interesting, meaningful, and memorable for my children, who were small at the time. I made the clothes and had help getting something sewn for me.

My family—my mother and sisters and their families—enjoyed the day more than usual. The holiday seemed more important to everyone, maybe because it felt as though we were enacting history.

But it's not just about trying to relive the period. Thanksgiving Day is special to me because I'm grateful for so many things, mostly that my family and I are together and that we're well. I'm grateful that we live in America. I'm grateful we can walk through the streets of a big city and dress how we want. I'm grateful we can pray how we want. And that's what Thanksgiving Day is all about.[9]

In recent times, many historians learned that the Puritans wore colorful clothes and were not limited to the black and white garments people associated with them. The idea of men wearing buckles on their hats and shoes are myths as well.[10]

◆ ◆ ◆ ◆

These symbols and traditions became linked with Thanksgiving over a long period of time.

However, new and more accurate facts have been discovered about its history. People also know that Thanksgiving Day is a day of sadness among many American Indians—especially the Wampanoag. The event now brings additional thought, sensitivity, and appreciation for a people who gave so much, but lost much more.

Thanksgiving Today

Thanksgiving Day is still about the main tradition started centuries ago—giving thanks for life's blessings over a big meal shared with family and friends. Many foods typically included in the holiday feast commemorate those native to North America and enjoyed by the early colonists: cranberry sauce, squash, corn, and pumpkin pie. In keeping with the custom, turkey is probably on the menu. Books and magazines are filled with recipes and ideas for leftover food. The president offers a Thanksgiving Day proclamation each year, a tradition started by George Washington.

However, there have been changes. Modern travel and technology allow quick connections to friends and family. Microwave ovens, better refrigeration for storage, and other appliances make food preparation easier and faster.

More information from historians has also become available that explains the holiday's beginnings more accurately. For many people, Thanksgiving Day will not be thought of in the same way again.

The Wampanoag

Today there are three Wampanoag communities, two in Massachusetts and one in Rhode Island. Although the residents live in modern homes, many still hunt, fish, and farm. They also follow the oral traditions of their ancestors—the people who came before them—which includes giving thanks for nature's gifts.

The Wampanoag speak English and accept Christianity as their religion. Following their tradition, they give their time to those who are less fortunate. But the Wampanoag have many regrets about the holiday, including how it focuses more on football and parades and less about heartfelt prayer and gratitude.

On Thanksgiving Day, the Wampanoag remember their past with pride, but with sadness, too. For centuries, many American Indians have been angry about the injustices done to their people. They remember how their troubles began with the arrival of European explorers, who carried diseases that killed so many American Indians. Others were kidnapped and sold as slaves.

The Wampanoag remember that their ancestors helped the Plymouth colonists, who would not have survived their first winter in New England without them. Books that give a wrong picture of American Indians and inaccurate facts also sadden the Wampanoag. For example, they do not believe that their ancestors were invited to the 1621 harvest festival. The Wampanoag also remember the land taken by the settlers who arrived years later, and how they mistreated the American Indians.

Since 1970, many Wampanoag have openly discussed their feelings about Thanksgiving Day. They call it a "Day of Mourning" and a time of great sadness. As Frank James, a Wampanoag spokesman, said about the holiday in 1972, "It is with a heavy heart that I look back at what happened to my people."[1]

For the past thirty years on Thanksgiving Day, a crowd of American Indians and people sympathetic to their cause have gathered at the statue of Massasoit overlooking Plymouth Rock. A group called United American Indians of New England organizes the event that includes a march through the historic district of Plymouth, Massachusetts.

Participants of the Day of Mourning may fast from sunset the day before through the afternoon of Thanksgiving Day. American Indians make speeches about their political and social concerns. Later that day, the group ends their fast with a shared meal that includes turkey, stuffing, vegetables, and fruit.[2]

The Wampanoag also remember the peace treaty between the settlers and the American Indians that lasted over fifty years. They hope that in the future there can be a better relationship between them and their fellow citizens.

Working toward that goal, many Wampanoag have helped historical groups and museum staff by contributing their point of view and their information about the early colonial period. They have also built their own project, the Mashpee Wampanoag Indian Museum located in Mashpee,

These American Indians gather together during a national Day of Mourning. The chief of the Pequot Wampanoag tribe, named Tall Oak, is standing center.

Massachusetts, near Plymouth Rock. Russell M. Peters, president of the Mashpee Wampanoag Indian Tribal Council, says of such efforts, "These are some of the positive ways in which we can balance the scale of history and establish pride in the Wampanoag identity and heritage."[3]

There would not have been a harvest festival in Plymouth had it not been for the Wampanoag. Their contributions to the holiday we now call Thanksgiving Day are a lasting part of American history and tradition. Their teachings—knowing how to farm, hunt, fish, and build houses—saved people and helped create a nation. Their generosity and helpfulness must not be forgotten.

Helping the Needy

Many people know that the word *giving* is an important part of the holiday's meaning and purpose. They donate food to needy people or help serve Thanksgiving Day dinners at homeless shelters.

Many charitable groups help thousands of needy people on Thanksgiving Day. The Salvation Army, a big international organization, began in London in 1865. It started in the United States in New York City in 1879. Today the Salvation Army has branches around the country and the world.

A big part of the Thanksgiving season is about helping others. These people are preparing dinners for people who are less fortunate.

Volunteers may serve a full dinner to homeless people at large places such as the YMCA. For those wishing to eat dinner at home, food baskets are available at certain locations.[4]

A Thanksgiving Cares program in Virginia also supplies holiday dinners to hundreds of under-privileged families in their region. Elsewhere, church groups and neighborhood organizations collect donations and serve meals at this time for those who are less fortunate.[5]

Macy's Thanksgiving Day Parade

A typical Macy's Thanksgiving Day Parade features bands from high schools nationwide, more than fifty huge balloons, and twelve thousand marchers. More than twenty floats carried performers who sang and waved to the 3 million people watching along the two-and-one-half-mile route. Millions of viewers saw the show on television.

Since 1999, there has been a float celebrating Indian culture and heritage. A performer wears an authentic headdress.

Preparation for the event takes place each year in a warehouse in New Jersey. On the day before Thanksgiving, trucks carry the floats into New York City. There, balloons are hooked to tankers and are pumped with helium, the gas that helps them rise.

During the parade, seventeen hundred balloon-handlers wear the same colors as the characters they are holding. Balloon-handlers are volunteers, who are usually Macy's workers and

Macy's Thanksgiving Day Parade features floats of well-known cartoon characters, like Charlie Brown.

their friends. On Thanksgiving Day, they report to the parade's starting point at five o'clock in the morning.

Balloons come in many different figures and have included favorite characters from comics and cartoons, such as Charlie Brown and SpongeBob SquarePants. As the parade's largest balloon, it is 62 feet high, 38 feet wide, and filled with 16,200 cubic feet of helium.[6]

About eight hundred people—the store's workers and their friends—volunteer as clowns for the parade. They attend a "clown camp" established especially for the event.[7]

Plymouth, Massachusetts

Plymouth—the oldest town in New England—has two museums dedicated to the Pilgrim era. One is Pilgrim Hall Museum, which has exhibits and displays items that belonged to the early colonists.

Another museum is Plimoth Plantation. The building began displaying exhibits in the 1940s. For over twenty years, the Wampanoag have contributed their time and information to many of the exhibits shown at the museum. Archeologists, people who dig in the earth for historical objects, have uncovered dozens of items belonging to the American Indians and the Pilgrims.

The museum features a 1627 Pilgrim village filled with homes and people wearing authentic costumes. They perform real chores, such as gathering crops, cooking, or watering a garden. Visitors may also see the actors enjoying a harvest feast.

These students look over the railing that now surrounds the famous Plymouth Rock near Plimouth Plantation in Massachusetts.

On Thanksgiving Day, many Plymouth citizens wear colonial costumes and walk to the local church to pray in an interfaith service. They believe that Plymouth is the home of America's first Thanksgiving, and they commemorate the day in the colonial New England tradition.[7]

Mayflower II

Historians are not sure what happened to the original ship after it returned to England in April 1621, but a copy, the *Mayflower II*, was built from 1955–1957. Funds were collected from the English people in a show of appreciation for America's help during World War II. A company in England made the vessel. As much as possible, the materials resemble those used in the 1600s.

The *Mayflower II* left Plymouth, England, on April 20, 1957. It sailed across the Atlantic Ocean for fifty-five days and landed at Plymouth Harbor on June 13, 1957. Thousands of people came to cheer the ship's arrival.

The *Mayflower II* is docked at Plimoth Plantation. Costumed actors on board the ship play the roles of the English voyagers and the ship's captain and crew. They discuss life aboard the vessel and their reasons for leaving England.

The *Mayflower II* is being pulled by a tugboat as it travels into Boston Harbor.

The boat can sail and has made voyages along the New England coast in recent years. It is safer than the original *Mayflower*. For example, a modern staircase connecting the main and lower decks has replaced the ladder used in the 1600s. *Mayflower II* also has electric lighting.[8]

Black Friday

Throughout history, when a bad event happened on a Friday, the day became known as Black Friday. But after World War II, Black Friday came to mean the day after Thanksgiving—when holiday gift shopping traditionally begins. The name commemorates a time when sales figures were recorded in ink. If a store showed a loss in sales, those numbers were written in red. If a store did well—showing a profit—figures were written in black. The day after Thanksgiving is often a good one for stores.

Although record-keeping has changed since the post-World War II era, the term *Black Friday* is still used by shopkeepers and the media. It is generally believed that the figures posted for that day's earnings will predict how well a store will do that season.[9]

In November 2005, about eighty stores in a Bakersfield, California, mall were open for business at two o'clock in the morning. Customers were there, waiting to shop.[10]

People have also used the Internet to buy holiday presents. The term *Black Monday* has come to reflect the heavy use of online shopping on the Monday after Thanksgiving. But according to

Internet trackers, Black Friday is still the busiest day for gift purchases.

Some people are angry about how the holiday season has become too much about gift giving. Beginning in the 1990s, they have tried to convince shoppers not to buy anything on Black Friday. They enter large stores and wheel around empty shopping carts while asking people not to spend their money. Over the years, the movement has spread to many countries, including Canada, Mexico, Japan, Great Britain, and the Netherlands.[11]

Turkey Bowl

Amateur football games called Turkey Bowls have sprung up across the Unites States in recent years. Teams play on Thanksgiving Day while their families, friends, and neighbors watch.

The first Turkey Bowl began in San Francisco in the mid-1940s, after high school competitions, the Academic Athletic Association championship, attracted big crowds on Thanksgiving Day.[12]

The term *Turkey Bowl* has grown to include other sports, too, such as bowling.

◆ ◆ ◆ ◆

One reason why Thanksgiving Day is special is because it started so long ago, but is still celebrated similarly—with people eating, visiting, and having fun. The day before the holiday has also become significant, with many people traveling to see friends and family or preparing for holiday guests.

But Thanksgiving Day in America is still mostly about helping to prepare a big feast and enjoying it. It is about spending time with loved ones. It is about helping others who are less fortunate. It is watching a big parade and cheering football teams. It is remembering the past and all those who paved the way. Most of all, Thanksgiving is being grateful for the present, and for living in a country where people can celebrate the day as they choose.

Help Out!

Celebrate the spirit of the Thanksgiving holiday by helping out. There are many things you can do, here are just a few. Ask an adult for permission or for help.

1. Find a soup kitchen in your town. Help give out food to those in need.

2. Find a local place of worship that is making turkey dinners. Ask how you could help.

3. Volunteer at a hospital and bring cheer to sick patients.

4. Organize a canned food drive in your neighborhood, then donate the cans to a local food pantry.

ancestors—Family members who lived many years ago.

bill—A written plan for a new law.

colonies—Settlements formed in a distant place by people who are still loyal to the leaders of their homeland.

commemorate—To serve as a reminder of something.

Congress—The lawmaking body of the United States government.

custom—The usual way of doing something.

descendants—Relatives who are born in later generations.

gratitude—A feeling of being thankful.

harvest—The gathering of crops.

immigrate—To move to another country to live.

mythology—A group of fictional or legendary stories set in the distant past. They feature heroes and gods who are used to explain a cultural practice or an unusual event.

persecution—Cruel and unfair treatment of a person or group, especially because of their racial or religious differences.

pilgrim—A person who travels to a distant land, mostly for religious reasons.

Puritans—Protestants who wanted to purify, or change, the Church of England, which combines Catholicism and Protestantism.

Separatists—Puritans who broke away from their country's main church, the Church of England.

shallop—A small sailboat carried on the *Mayflower*. Passengers used it to explore shallow waters along the Massachusetts coastline.

tolerance—The acceptance of people who are different, particularly in race, religion, and nationality.

tradition—A custom or belief that has existed for a long time.

treaty—A formal agreement between two or more groups.

CHAPTER NOTES

Chapter 1. Grateful Neighbors

1. Richard Archer, *Fissures in the Rock: New England in the Seventeenth Century* (Hanover, N.H.: University Press of New England, 2001), p. 8.

2. Alden T. Vaughen, *New England Frontier: Puritans and Indians, 1620–1675* (Boston: Little, Brown, and Co. 1965), p. 84.

3. Edward Winslow, *Good Newes from New England*, first published in 1624 in London (Bedford, reprinted by Applewood Books), pp. 31–37.

Chapter 2. Holiday Beginnings

1. Jessica Faust and Jacky Sach, *The Book of Thanksgiving: Stories, Poems, and Recipes for Sharing One of America's Greatest Holidays* (New York: Citadel Press, 2002), pp. 154–155.

2. Sue Ellen Thompson, *Holiday Symbols and Customs*, 3rd ed. (Detroit: Omnigraphics, 2003), pp. 710–714.

3. Ibid., pp. 157–158.

4. Kathleen Curtin, Sandra L. Oliver, and Plimoth Plantation, *Giving Thanks: Thanksgiving Recipes and History, from Pilgrims to Pumpkin Pie*, (New York: Clarkson Potter, 2005), p. 14.

5. Diana Karter Appelbaum, *Thanksgiving: An American Holiday, An American History* (New York: Facts On File, 1984), pp. 14–17.

6. Francis Dillon, *The Pilgrims* (Garden City, N.Y.: Doubleday, 1975), p. 6.

7. Ibid., pp. 67–69.

8. Ibid., pp. 77–86.

9. Ibid., pp. 89–102.

10. Eugene Aubrey Stratton, *Plymouth Colony: Its History and People, 1620–1691* (Salt Lake City: Ancestry Publishing, 1986), p. 18.

11. Alan Axelrod, and Charles Phillips, *What Every American Should Know About American History*, 2nd ed. (Avon: Adams Media, 2004), pp. 6–7.

12. Dillon, pp. 134–135.

13. Pauline Maier, "Plymouth Company," *World Book Online Reference Center*, n.d., <http://www.aolsvc.worldbook.aol.com/wb/Article> (January 24, 2005).

14. Dillon, pp. 117–130.

15. Edward Bleier, *The Thanksgiving Ceremony* (New York: Crown Publishing, 2003), pp. 30–31.

16. Judy Dow and Beverly Slapin, "Deconstructing the Myths of 'The First Thanksgiving,'" *Multicultural Review*, Fall 2004, p. 47.

17. Curtin et al., p. 19.

18. Dillon, pp. 136–138.

19. Dillon, pp. 143–149.

20. Pilgrim Hall Museum, "Plymouth Rock in the 17th Century," n.d., <http://www.pilgrimhall.org/Rock.htm> (January 30, 2005).

21. Dillon, pp. 150–152.

22. Alden T. Vaughan, *New England Frontier: Puritans and Indians, 1620–1675* (Boston: Little, Brown, and Co. 1965), p. 68.

23. Bill Bigelow and Bob Peterson, eds., *Rethinking Thanksgiving* (Milwaukee, Wisc.: Rethinking Schools, 1998), pp. 76–78.

24. Dillon, pp. 153–156.

25. Faust and Sach, pp. 6–9.

26. Stratton, pp. 21–22.

27. "Modern Translation of Edward Winslow's Letter," Plimoth Plantation, Online Learning Center, n.d., <http://www.plimoth.org/OLC/Primary_Source _Winslow_text.pdf> (January 30, 2005).

28. Curtin et al., p. 15.

29. Ibid., pp. 17–18

30. Ibid., pp. 21–22.

31. Ibid., p. 22.

32. Ibid., p. 26.

33. Faust and Sach, p. 9.

34. Curtin et al., p. 27.

35. Eric B. Schultz and Michael J. Tougias, *King Philip's War: The History and Legacy of America's Forgotten Conflict* (Woodstock, N.Y.: The Countryman Press, 1999), pp. 22–23.

36. Axelrod and Philips, pp. 19–20.

37. Schultz and Tougias, p. 2.

38. James D. Drake, *King Philip's War: Civil War in New England, 1675–1676* (Amherst, Mass.: University of Massachusetts Press, 1999), pp. 91–93.

39. Ibid., pp. 119–120.

40. Alan Taylor, *American Colonies*, Eric Foner, ed. (New York: Viking, 2001), pp. 201–202.

41. Appelbaum, p. 46.
42. Faust and Sach, pp. 10–11.
43. Pilgrim Hall Museum, "National Thanksgiving Proclamations," July 14, 1998, <http://www.pilgrim hall.org/ThanxProc.htm> (April 4, 2006).
44. Faust and Sach, p. 38.
45. Ibid., p. 153.
46. Ibid., pp. 243–244.

◆ Chapter 3. Cultural Contributions

1. Kathleen Curtin, Sandra L. Oliver, and Plimoth Plantation, *Giving Thanks: Thanksgiving Recipes and History, from Pilgrims to Pumpkin Pie* (New York: Clarkson Potter, 2005), p. 22.
2. Louisa May Alcott, *An Old Fashioned Thanksgiving* (Whitefish: Kessinger Publishing, 2004).
3. Orange County Mayflower Colony, "Pilgrim Paintings," 1999, n.d., <http://www.ocmayflower.org/pilgrim2.htm> (February 20, 2005).
4. Pilgrim Hall Museum, "Embarkation of the Pilgrims," n.d., <http://www.pilgrimhall.org/hpweir.htm> (December 5, 2005).
5. "Grandma Moses," March 2, 2003, <http://www.rootsweb.com/~nyrensse/bio500.htm> (April 7, 2006).
6. Laura Claridge, *Norman Rockwell: A Life* (New York: Random House, 2001), p. 65.
7. The Norman Rockwell Museum at Stockbridge, "Norman Rockwell: A Brief Biography," 2005, <http://www.nrm.org/norman/> (January 30, 2006).
8. Edward Bleier, *The Thanksgiving Ceremony* (New York: Crown Publishing, 2003), p. 116.

9. Ibid., p. 111.

10. Curtin et al., pp. 116–117.

11. Linda Murray Berzok, *American Indian Food* (Westport, Conn.: Greenwood Press, 2005), p. 60.

12. Ibid., p. 38.

13. Ibid., pp. 124–125.

14. Curtin et al., p. 49.

15. Sue Ellen Thompson, *Holiday Symbols and Customs*, 3rd ed. (Detroit: Omnigraphics, 2003), pp. 267–268.

16. Appelbaum, pp. 198–200.

17. Curtin, et al., p. 53.

18. Robert Sullivan, *America's Parade: A Celebration of Macy's Thanksgiving Day Parade* (New York: Life Books/Time, Inc. 2001), pp. 10–11.

19. Robert M. Grippo and Christopher Hoskins, *Macy's Thanksgiving Day Parade* (Chicago: Arcadia Publishing, 2004), p. 11.

20. Ibid., p. 21.

◆ Chapter 4. Thanksgiving Around the World

1. Personal interview with Peggy Baker, curator and director of the Pilgrim Hall Museum, November 10, 2005.

2. "Cranberry Day," Wampanoag Tribe—Other Stories and Information, <http://www.wampanoagtribe.net/Pages/Wampanoag_Way/other> (December 2, 2005).

3. Jessica Faust and Jacky Sach, *The Book of Thanksgiving: Stories, Poems, and Recipes for Sharing One of America's Greatest Holidays* (New York: Citadel Press, 2002), pp. 154–155.

Chapter Notes

4. Carol Stepanchuk and Charles Wong, *Mooncakes and Hungry Ghosts: Festivals of China* (San Francisco: China Books, 1991), pp. 51–55.
5. Faust and Sach, pp. 157–158.
6. Ibid., p. 158.
7. "Yam Festival in Africa," n.d., *Harvest Festival in Africa*, <http://www.pongalfestival.org/yam-festival-africa.html> (December 19, 2005).
8. "Pongal: The Harvest Festival of South India," n.d., <http://www.pongalfestival.org/the-harvest-festival.html> (January 30, 2006).
9. Ask Asia, "Chusok: The Korean Thanksgiving," n.d., <http://www.askasia.org/teachers/essays/essay.php?no=2&era=&grade=&geo=> (January 30, 2006).
10. "English Festivals," Harvest Festivals From Around the World, n.d., <http://www.harvestfestivals.net/englishfestivals.htm> (December 12, 2005).

◆ **Chapter 5. Holiday Symbols**

1. Sue Ellen Thompson, *Holiday Symbols and Customs*, 3rd ed. (Detroit: Omnigraphics, Inc., 2003), p. 748.
2. Kathleen Curtin, Sandra L. Oliver, and Plimoth Plantation, *Giving Thanks: Thanksgiving Recipes and History, from Pilgrims to Pumpkin Pie* (New York: Clarkson Potter, 2005), p. 46.
3. The White House, "Turkey," n.d., <http://www.whitehouse.gov/holiday/Thanksgiving/2005> (November 22, 2005).
4. Thompson, p. 745.
5. Plimoth Plantation, "Glossary," n.d., <http://www.plimoth.org/learn/history/glossary.asp> (January 30, 2005).

6. Jerry Baskin, "Gourd," *World Book Online Reference Center*, World Book, Inc., n.d., <http://www.aolsvc. worldbook.aol.com/wb/article?id=ar230820> (February 19, 2005).

7. B. J. Welborn, *America's Best Historic Sites: 101 Terrific Places to Take the Family* (Chicago: Chicago Review Press, 1998), pp. 22–23.

8. "Massasoit," n.d., <http://www.geocities.com/dl_ hubbard/massasoit.html> (November 29, 2005).

9. Personal interview with Gail Propp, November 22, 2005.

10. Robert Jennings Heinsohn, "Sail 1620—Discover History: Pilgrim Clothing," n.d., <http://www.sail 1620.org/discover_feature_pilgrim_clothing.shtml> (December 5, 2005).

◆ Chapter 6. Thanksgiving Today

1. The Children's Museum, "What You Need to Know— Wampanoag Life After 1620," n.d., <http://www. bostonkids.org/educators/wampanoag/html/ w-thanks.htm> (February 13, 2005).

2. United American Indians of New England, "National Day of Mourning," n.d., <http://home.earthlink. net/~uainendom/> (January 30, 2006).

3. Pilgrim Hall Museum, "National Day of Mourning," n.d., <http://www.pilgrimhall.org/daymourn.htm> (January 30, 2006).

4. Salvation Army—History, n.d., <http://www. salvationarmy-georgia.org/history.htm> (December 19, 2005).

5. Arlo Wagner, "Volunteers Pack Dinners in a Box for Families in Need," n.d., *Washington, D.C. Times*, November 22, 2005.

6. John Crudele, "Pulling Strings," *New York Post*, November 22, 2005, pp. 48–50.

7. Reed Tucker, "System of a Clown," *New York Post*, November 22, 2005, p. 52.

8. Diana Karter Appelbaum, *Thanksgiving: An American Holiday, An American History* (New York: Facts on File, 1984) p. 264.

9. Plimoth Plantation, *"Mayflower II,"* n.d., <http://www.plimoth.org/visit/what/mayflower2.asp> (November 22, 2005).

10. Hennig Cohen and Tristram Potter Coffin, eds., *Folklore of American Holidays* (Detroit: Gale Publishing, 1987), p. 353.

11. Ryan Schuster, "Stores to Open at 2 A.M. on Black Friday," *Bakersfield Californian* (November 17, 2005).

12. "Buy Nothing Day," n.d., <http://adbusters.org/metas/eco/bnd/blog.php> (December 2, 2005).

13. Jim Gigliotti, "High school football a Turkey Day Tradition," NFL.com—Thanksgiving Classic, n.d., <http://www.nfl.com/features/thanksgiving/high_school_football> (February 25, 2005).

FURTHER READING

Books

Davis, Ken C. *Don't Know Much About the Pilgrims*. New York: HarperCollins, 2002.

O'Neill, Catherine Grace, and Margaret M. Bruchac with Plimoth Plantation. *1621: A New Look at Thanksgiving.* Washington, D.C.: National Geographic Society, 2001.

Landau, Elaine. *Celebrate the First Thanksgiving with Elaine Landau.* Berkeley Heights, N.J.: Enslow Publishers, Inc., 2006.

Santella, Andrew. *The First Thanksgiving.* New York: Children's Press, 2003.

Williams, Gianna, and Janet Riehecky. *The Plymouth Colony.* Milwaukee, Wisc.: Gareth Stevens Pub., 2002.

Internet Addresses

Pilgrim Hall Museum
  <http://www.pilgrimhall.org>
  Learn more about the Pilgrims and early American history.

Plimoth Plantation
  <http://www.plimoth.org>
  Plimoth Plantation is "living breathing history." Visit their Web site for more information about the Pilgrims and American Indians.

INDEX

A

American Revolution, 34–35, 78

Autumn Moon Festival, 62–63

B

Baker, Peggy, 60

Black Friday, 96–97

Bradford, William, 6–7, 12, 15, 17, 25, 27, 28, 29, 44, 77

Brewster, William, 12

Browne, Robert, 11–12

C

Canada, 10, 24, 61–62, 69

Carver, John, 13–14, 19, 25, 26

Child, Lydia Maria, 48, 50

Chusok, 67

Congress, 35, 41

corn, 18, 19, 26, 27, 50, 74–75, 83

cornucopia, 73–74

Cranberry Day, 60–61

Curtin, Kathleen, 74

F

"first" thanksgiving, the, 27, 50, 53

football, 53, 54–55

G

Great Swamp Fight, 33

H

Hale, Sarah, 39

harvest home festival, 27, 68–69

J

Jones, Christopher, 16, 17, 22

K

King George III, 34–35

King James I, 11, 12

King Philip's War, 32–34

L

Lincoln, Abraham, 38, 40

M

Macy's Thanksgiving Day Parade, 55, 57, 90, 92

Massasoit, 5–7, 25, 29–30, 32, 78–79
Mayflower, 15–17, 19, 21, 22, 30, 44, 45, 77–78
Mayflower II, 94–95
Mayflower Compact, 19

N
Narragansett tribe, 22, 23, 32, 33

P
Philip (Metacom), 32–34
Pilgrims, 44–45, 46, 79
Pilgrim Hall Museum, 92
Plimoth Plantation, 28, 92–93
Plymouth Rock, 21, 77–78
Pongal, 66–67
Propp, Gail, 79–81
Puritans, 11, 27–28, 36, 51, 81

R
Rockwell, Norman, 47–48
Roosevelt, Franklin D., 40–41

S
"Saints", 15, 17, 27
Samoset, 23

Second Continental Congress, 35
Separatists, 11, 12–14, 15, 17, 23, 44
Speedwell, 15, 46
Squanto (Tisquantum), 23, 24, 25–26, 50
Standish, Miles, 15, 18, 29
"Strangers", 15, 17, 26
Sukkot, 10, 63–65

T
Thursday, 36, 39, 40, 41
tofu, 53
turkey, 30, 36, 50, 53, 59, 71-73, 83
Turkey Bowl, 97–98

W
Wampanoag tribe, 5, 7, 18, 19, 22–23, 25, 26, 29, 30, 32, 33, 53, 60, 78, 79, 80, 81, 84–86, 88, 92
Wamsutta (Alexander), 32
Washington, George, 35, 84
Winslow, Edward, 5–7, 28, 44, 45, 77

Y
Yam Festival, 66